New Zealand

New Zealand

PHOTOGRAPHS

Eric Taylor

TEXT

Michael King

HODDER AND STOUGHTON
AUCKLAND LONDON SYDNEY TORONTO

ACKNOWLEDGEMENT

The people who helped in the making of this book – providing advice, transport, accommodation and photographic subjects – are too numerous to name individually. But I offer them all my heart-felt thanks for their companionship and for the confidence they showed in the outcome of this project.

Eric Taylor

Book design by Donna Hoyle, Auckland.
Typesetting by Ay & Jay Typesetters, Auckland.
Printed and bound in Hong Kong for Hodder and
Stoughton Ltd, 44-46 View Road, Glenfield, Auckland,
New Zealand.

Introduction

In the beginning was the land. And the land was without people. It was without people, in fact, longer than any habitable continent or major island on earth.

At the time of the formation of its oldest surfaces some 500 million years ago, New Zealand was part of the great southern supercontinent of Gondwanaland. It lay wedged against the geological formation that would eventually become Antarctica. Two hundred and twenty million years later it was separated from Gondwanaland but retained natural bridges to other land masses. It was from this time that the ancestors of life forms that would later be unique to the country – ferns, podocarps, tuatara, moa and kiwi – began to migrate there.

From 65 to five million years ago, New Zealand was on its own and immensely volatile. Parts of it reared from and plunged back into the sea, joined, separated, and joined again. It was a continuation of this activity in addition to volcanic explosions, the presence of active earthquake fault lines, glacial scouring and erosion that produced the landscape that human inhabitants would eventually value for its extraordinary variety.

The whole northern peninsula of the North Island derives from one of the major wrinkles in the earth's crust that appears further north in the island chain of New Caledonia. A second wrinkle forms the mountain chain that runs diagonally from the East Cape of the North Island down to the Southern Alps. The convergence of these wrinkles around the central North Island produced one of the country's most arresting features: the volcanic plateau with its combination of mountains, lakes, geysers and silica formations. Some of the greatest eruptions on the earth's surface originated on this plateau. And they altered the New Zealand landscape over thousands of square kilometres. The most recent was the Taupo eruption of about AD135, which created the largest lake in the country and threw ash so high into the atmosphere that it was detected as far away as China and Rome. Some New Zealand volcanoes, such as Taranaki, Tarawera and Rangitoto, were active until the phase of human settlement. Others, such as Ruapehu, Ngauruhoe and White Island, are active still. The last major eruption to extinguish life on a large scale was that of Mount Tarawera in 1886.

South and east of the volcanic plateau rise mountainous ranges thrown up less than five million years ago. They subsequently developed sharp ridges and deep valleys as a consequence of erosion. Impressive headlands that extend like fingers to the coast in the south of the North Island were produced by fault lines – breaks in the earth's crust caused by massive compression. Some faults are active still and produce periodic earthquakes, of which the last serious ones were those in Napier in 1931 and the Bay of Plenty in 1987.

Across Cook Strait, formed some 10,000 years ago, fault lines continue in huge uplifted ranges that run from the Kaikouras in the north of the island to the Southern Alps chain that dominates the West Coast. Here 19 peaks exceed 3,000 metres (Ruapehu, the highest in the North Island, is only 2,797 metres) and the largest is Mt Cook at 3,764 metres. An accumulation of snow in the alps formed massive glaciers that slid down the eastern and western sides of the ranges. The effect was to create what would become the most stunning scenery in the country: grooved valleys and long-fingered lakes. Shingle gathered and carried forward by the glaciers was further moved by rivers to create the lowlands on the east of the South Island, including the vast, flat Canterbury Plains. Retreating remnants of those glaciers are still visible in surviving ice floes, such as the Tasman and the Franz Josef.

Climate too contributed to the eventual shape and appearance of the South Island. Rain falls evenly over the north of the country, but it is distributed disproportionately in the south: the West Coast and south-west regions have one of the heaviest rainfalls in the world; Marlborough, Canterbury and Central Otago contain semi-arid basins among the hills, apparent in the spread of desert-like tussock grass. The eastern districts of the island are in general warmer and drier than those to the west.

The people who eventually found this empty land, inhabited only by birds, bats and insects, were Polynesian: descendants of Austronesian tribes who had abandoned the mainland of South-East Asia some 6,000 years before. Arriving by canoe some 1,200 years ago they brought with them a complex set of traditions that allowed them to explain their existence and that of the land before them.

In the beginning, their mythology told them, was Te Kore, the Void. After a series of evolutionary convulsions which produced successive epochs of darkness and light, Te Kore gave rise to Rangi the Sky Father and Papa the Earth Mother, who came together in conjugal embrace. This embrace begat offspring. But it left the world between the parents in perpetual darkness. The sons of Rangi and Papa constantly lamented the miserable conditions in which they were forced to live. Eventually they resolved to do something. One, Tu-matauenga, god of war, suggested that the parents would have to be killed to be separated. Tane-mahuta, god of the forest and later father of mankind, objected. No, he said. It would be sufficient to prise them apart and let the Sky stand above and the Earth lie below. Let the Sky become a stranger but the Earth remain the nurturing Mother.

All but one of the sons agreed to this course and took turns trying to bring about the separation. None succeeded until Tane-mahuta placed his shoulders against the Earth and his feet upon the Sky. Slowly and powerfully he straightened his body and his parents reluctantly gave way. The sinews with which they held each other tore and they cried out in pain. But Tane persisted. And in the end he succeeded in fixing the Sky above and the Earth below. As soon as this was done the children of Rangi and Papa knew light for the first time. And the children of Tane – the trees, birds and insects of the forest – were able to breathe, to see and to move.

The one son who had objected to the separation, Tawhiri-matea, was angered by the pain his parents had suffered and the regard in which Tane-mahuta was now held by other living things. So he followed Rangi to the realm above and produced his own offspring: wind, rain and storms. He unleashed these on the children of Tane in retribution. He then hurled himself down from the skies as a hurricane and uprooted Tane's trees. Eventually, after attacking all his brothers, Tawhiri-matea returned to the Sky, from where he and his children continue to descend from time to time to plague the Earth and her occupants.

It was Tane-mahuta who then created the first woman out of earth and procreated with her. Their descendants, who also procreated, produced a line of men-like gods and god-like men. One of these, Maui, was credited with fishing up the North Island of New Zealand – an especially appropriate myth in the light of the island's relatively recent volcanic history. Maui was an archetypal hero throughout Polynesia. He was the last-born in his family so that in theory his rank was low. But he compensated for this by being far more resourceful and imaginative than his brothers.

In the fish story (and there are many others) Maui smuggled himself aboard his brothers' canoe in Hawaiki, the traditional Polynesian homeland. They were annoyed by his trickery and wanted to return to shore. But by this time land was too far away so they continued with their planned fishing expedition. After the brothers had filled the canoe with their catch Maui produced his own hook, the barb of which was made from a fragment of his grandmother's jaw-bone. The brothers refused him bait so Maui struck his own nose and smeared the hook with blood. He lowered his line and almost immediately hooked a fish of incredible magnitude. The only way he could haul it up was by reciting a chant to make heavy weights light.

When the great fish had at last reached the surface Maui left the canoe to find a priest who could make an offering to the gods and perform the appropriate ritual. He warned his brothers not to touch the mighty creature until this was done. The brothers, however, ignored him. They leapt from the canoe and began to scale the fish and to hack at its flesh. The fish raised its fins and writhed in agony. The sun rose and made the flesh solid underfoot, its surface rough and mountainous because of the brothers' mutilation. It remained that way. And the name given to it was Te Ika-a-Maui, the fish of Maui.

The name for the South Island was drawn from its jade deposits: Te Wai Pounamu, greenstone water; or Te Waahi Pounamu, place of greenstone. The story of its origin told by the Ngai Tahu people who occupied it was a variation of the creation myth. According to their account, Rangi the Sky Father had a union with Pohato-te-po before being joined with Papa. One of the children of this first marriage was Aorangi, rendered Aoraki in southern dialect. Aoraki and his brothers were opposed to the second marriage. In protest they left Hawaiki by canoe. In the vicinity of the South Island, however, their vessel struck a submerged reef and was wrecked. Aoraki and his brothers climbed to the higher side of the canoe so as not to drown. They waited so long for rescue that they turned to stone and became the Southern Alps. Aoraki or Mt Cook, the eldest, is the highest of the peaks; the others are the remaining brothers in descending order of seniority according to size. In this version, the Place of Greenstone is actually Te Waka-a-Aoraki, Aoraki's canoe. The Marlborough Sounds at the northern end represent the shattered prow; and Bluff Hill in the far south is the stern. The broken ranges of Southland and Otago are the jumbled remains of the vessel's cargo. Stewart Island (Rakiura) is the anchor stone.

The land that the ancestors of the Maori discovered some 1,200 years ago was unlike anything that Polynesians had encountered elsewhere in the Pacific. It was far larger – more than 1,500 kilometres north to south with a total area of nearly 270,000 square kilometres – and more varied than the islands they had colonised previously. It was temperate rather than tropical and sufficiently cold in much of the South Island to prevent the growing of crops. Other than bats, there were no land mammals until the Polynesian colonists released the rats and dogs they had brought with them. It is probable that they also brought pigs and fowls, but these did not survive.

The lack of meat was compensated for by a proliferation of seafood: fish, shellfish, crayfish, crab, seaweed, sea-egg and the sea mammals – whales, dolphins and seals. The land provided fern root that offered a staple food (though it had to be heavily pounded), and there were nearly 200 species of bird, many of them edible. Inland waterways contained additional resources: waterfowl, eel, fish and more shellfish. To all these the immigrants added the cultivated vegetables they had carried with them: taro, kumara, yam, gourds and the paper mulberry. For meat, in addition to birds, fish and sea mammals, there were limited supplies of dog and rat. Human flesh, a Maori anthropologist has noted, was eaten 'when procurable'.

The New Zealand forests offered larger trees than Polynesians had seen previously, in particular the giant kauri, kahikatea and totara. With these they built bigger dugout canoes and evolved a complex tradition of carving. Later they used wooden beams in the construction of dwellings. Materials such as raupo and nikau made excellent house walls and roofs. Flax plaited well into cords and baskets and provided fine fibre for garments. There was an ample sufficiency of suitable stone materials for adzes, chisels and drill points, varieties of bone for fish-hooks, spear-heads and ornaments, and obsidian for flake knives. Through these artifacts and crafts the New Zealand Polynesians developed one of the world's most sophisticated neolithic cultures.

Perhaps the most spectacular of the new country's resources was the huge flightless bird, the moa. There were originally some 24 species of this bird, ranging from the turkey-sized *Anomalopteryx* to the gigantic *Dinornis maximus*. They offered a food supply on a scale never before encountered in Polynesia (drumsticks the size of bullocks' legs) other than when whales were cast ashore. Some early groups of Maoris based their economy around moas in areas where the birds were relatively plentiful, until extensive exploitation led to their extinction.

The history of the first colonists from the time of their arrival until the advent of Europeans is a history of their adaptation to this environment – the matching of their skills and cultural resources to it, and the evolution of new features in their culture in response to the conditions that the environment imposed.

Ethnologists now recognise two distinct but related phases in that culture. The first is New Zealand East Polynesian, or Archaic Maori, represented by the archaeological remains of the earliest settlers and their immediate descendants. The second is Classic Maori, the culture encountered and recorded by the earliest European navigators to reach the country. The process by which the first phase evolved into the second is complex, and one on which scholars have not yet reached agreement.

What can be said with confidence, however, is that by the time James Cook and his men observed New Zealand in 1769, New Zealand Polynesians had settled the land from the far north to Foveaux Strait in the south. The language these inhabitants spoke was similar enough for a speaker to be understood anywhere in the country, although dialectal differences were pronounced, particularly between the North and South Islands. While regional variations were apparent in the details and traditions of the culture, the most important features of it were practised from one end of the country to the other.

Maori views of the land on which they lived were conditioned by the myth of Rangi and Papa. Papatuanuku, the Earth Mother, represented the womb and nurturer of humanity. For this reason the earth was respected and any modification of her contours preceded by prayers of propitiation. Similarly the resources were husbanded with care: fruits, fish, shellfish, birds, cultivated vegetables – all were taken in season and in such quantity as to ensure the resource was renewable. When items became scarce, a rahui or prohibition was declared to allow them to regenerate.

Mountains, hills, rivers and lakes were believed to be dwelling places of atua and tupuna – gods and ancestors. They were also seen as repositories of tribal and personal mana and were similarly treated with respect. The most sacred sites were tapu and could only be visited after the performance of appropriate ritual.

As their Polynesian ancestors had done, Maoris became intensely attached to the region in which they were born and grew up. The fact that their ancestors were likely to be buried there added to the strength of that attachment. When population pressure, defeat in warfare or a depletion of food resources forced people to move from their traditional homes to a new one, there would be much weeping over familiar landmarks and singing of waiata to lament departure. One such song, composed by the Maori King Tawhiao, encapsulates these attitudes and values:

I look down on the valley of Waikato,
As though to hold it in the hollow of my hand
And caress its beauty
Like some verdant thing.
I reach out from the top of Pirongia
As though to cover and protect its substance
With my own.
See how it bursts through
The full bosoms of Mangatautari and Maungakawa,
Hills of my inheritance:
The river of life, each curve

More beautiful than the last.
Across the smooth belly of Kirikiriroa,
Its gardens bursting with the fullness of good things,
Towards the meeting place at Ngaruawahia.
There on the fertile mount I would rest my head
And look through the thighs of Taupiri.
There at the place of all creation
Let the King come forth.

Such were the contours of Maori life that Cook and other European navigators encountered towards the end of the eighteenth century. The population was probably somewhere between 100,000 and 120,000. The Maori people had no concept of culture, nationhood or race, having been so long separated from other races and cultures. They were tribal beings who were fiercely assertive of the identity that they took from their ancestry and from their hapu membership. Most of them felt as far removed from Maoris to whom they were not related as they did from the Europeans who were soon to invade their country.

Cook's voyages, following that of Dutchman Abel Janzoon Tasman in 1642, put New Zealand literally and figuratively on the world map. Consequently, from the late eighteenth century, the country was also on the routes of European and North American vessels that found their way to the South Pacific. Sealers and whalers visited in large numbers and set up stations on the coast. Ships, largely from the neighbouring colony of New South Wales, came to harvest timber and flax. A substantial settlement grew around Kororareka in the Bay of Islands to service these vessels and to provide comfort and distraction for their crews. It attracted some of the worst elements of eighteenth- and nineteenth-century seagoing riff-raff. Life there was rugged and lawless, with special emphasis given to the delights of alcohol and sex.

Inevitably Christian missionaries followed, attracted by a potential harvest of heathen souls and shocked by the excesses of their fellow Europeans who had preceded them. After a slow start Maoris did embrace Christianity, and they welcomed especially literary, horticultural and agricultural training which came as part of the package of 'civilisation'. There was a period in the mid-1840s when the rate of literacy was higher among Maoris than it was among Europeans in New Zealand.

Organised colonisation by Europeans, now known collectively to the Maori as Pakeha, began in the late 1830s. The Wakefield family's New Zealand Company established settlements at Wellington, Nelson, Wanganui and New Plymouth. A French colony was founded at Akaroa on Banks Peninsula. Subsequently church settlements were begun in Dunedin (Scottish, Presbyterian) and Christchurch (Church of England). The growing number of British residents, the prospect of still more, the problems of law and order, fears for the welfare of the Maori – all these factors had led to the despatch of Lieutenant-Governor William Hobson from New South Wales to New Zealand in 1840, and to the signing of the Treaty of Waitangi, by which Maoris ceded sovereignty of the country to the British crown.

By the 1860s the number of Pakeha colonists exceeded that of the indigenous inhabitants. The new-comers made their influence visible on the landscape. They destroyed vast tracts of forest to extract timber for export and for the building of their cities, and to clear the way for the large-scale pastoral farming that was to be the source of the country's wealth for the next century. They ripped gold from the earth in Otago and on the West Coast and Coromandel Peninsula and left massive tailings of inert soil in their wake. In the twentieth century they replaced native timber with exotic pine and covered much of the central North Island with this renewable timber resource (Kaingaroa pine plantation, covering more than 4,000 square kilometres, is the largest man-made forest in the world).

Most visibly, the new colonists built their villages, towns and cities, and in doing so they set about transplanting the United Kingdom landscape they remembered in New Zealand's (to them) less hospitable soil. They erected English-style village churches surrounded by graveyards. They grew poplars and willows on their farms, fruit trees and English flowers around their homes. They introduced sparrows, thrushes and blackbirds, deer and rabbits. A book published in 1857 told would-be immigrants:

> When Christchurch has grown to a pretty town, and the young oak of England stands by the side of the trees indigenous to New Zealand, when the avenues to houses are lined by graceful and beautiful shrubs, when the green grass of England is sprouting in her meadows, fenced by hawthorn hedges, when daisies and buttercups flower over the land, when the timid hare springs across the field, and the coveys of partridges break from their cover, and the sun of heaven shines brightly through the pure atmosphere, tempered by breezes from the Pacific and the Alpine range, then there will be but one thing lacking to make New Zealand the Eden of the world – the charm of age, the vestiges of the past, the spot endeared by old associations and traditions.

The new colonists were trying, as the Maori had done before them, to make themselves at home. But the word 'Home' was reserved for England. As far as England was concerned, New Zealand could not have been more distant. It is the proverbial antipodes in relation to the Old World. An English poet, writing about her son going to visit his father in New Zealand, says 'he could go no further'. And Cook in the eighteenth century felt that his visit to the southern part of the Pacific had taken him 'as far as a man may go'. Europe did, in fact, come to New Zealand in the nineteenth and twentieth centuries. But neither Pakeha colonists nor Europeans who remained in Europe became any less conscious of the distance that separated the immigrants from the source of their Diaspora. Home-grown New Zealand literature voiced a feeling of rootlessness and isolation. Poet Allen Curnow lamented 'what great gloom stands in a land of settlers with never a soul at home'.

In times of global war, of course, the Pakeha feeling of isolation was even more acute, the supply lines to Europe stretched even more precariously. Another poet, R.A.K. Mason, was conscious of this when he spoke of being:

> ...here in this far-pitched perilous hostile place
> this solitary hard-assaulted spot
> fixed at the friendless outer edge of space.

Almost all early Pakeha observations of the New Zealand landscape located it on the periphery of a metropolitan or European vision, even when they gave it credit for great variety and beauty. G.B. Earp, for example:

It would seem as if nature, isolating this country from the great continents, had atoned for its banishment by concentrating within it all the varied features and resources which lie so widely apart in the more extensive surfaces of the earth. It has its Alpine districts, snow-clad and bristling with glaciers, whose drainage, falling in foaming cataracts, is received into numerous, and some of them considerable rivers; its table lands and plains, sometimes flat, at others undulated by rounded and fertile hills. Valleys overspread with rich verdure; and forests, the trees of which occasionally rise to a height that leaves no similarity between them and the tallest pines of Norway, also combine to form the scenery of New Zealand. Nor are the more forbidding aspects and phenomena of nature wanting. The mountains on the eastern side of the North Island contain volcanoes, some of the plateaux are cleft by yawning fissures of unfathomed depth, and the south-western coast presents the inhospitable faces of craggy and stupendous rocks. So dreary and desolate is the north extremity of these islands that the natives have fixed upon it as their 'Styx' leading to the abodes of the dead.

By the middle of the twentieth century, New Zealand was a geographical and historical paradox. Its inhabitants were of largely European stock (78 percent). Its location was Pacific. And its nearest powerful neighbours were Asian, a fact that scared many New Zealanders. After a fear of Russian invasion faded in the late nineteenth century, a feeling grew that New Zealand's fertile underpopulated land was attractive to and vulnerable to attack from an over-populated Asia. The fear took shape in World War Two when Japan launched its invasions into the Pacific. This trauma was followed by the realisation that the British Navy, on whom New Zealand had always depended as an international police force, could never reach the South Pacific in an emergency. In the event it was the United States who bailed New Zealand out in the Battles of Midway and the Coral Sea.

After World War Two New Zealand's feelings of isolation and insecurities took new forms. The dependence on Britain for defence was transferred to the United States in a series of regional defence pacts and joint military actions in Korea and Vietnam. For a time, the emergence of a communist government in China provided a new focal point for the old Yellow Peril fear, and the ultimate containment of China was a major reason cited for New Zealand's presence in Vietnam. Britain was still seen as the Mother Country and remained the destination for the bulk of New Zealand's exports.

In the 1960s and 1970s this too began to change. New Zealand politicians and diplomats began to explore the possibility that Asian neighbours might actually be potential friends. Overtures were made to Malaysia, Indonesia, Indo-China, Japan and, eventually, even to China. This process was given impetus by the determination of the EEC countries to shut New Zealand out of the European agricultural market. New Zealand began to seek new markets for her produce in Asia and slowly to find them, initially in Japan. Politicians began to speak of New Zealand as part of Asia, and a Labour Prime Minister promoted the idea in the early 1970s that countries interdependent through trade were unlikely to go to war – that friendly trading relations with one's neighbours, in other words, were likely to be the best guarantee of security.

The next Labour administration reversed even further the traditional patterns of loyalties and alliances. In the mid-1980s the New Zealand government declared the country nuclear-free and refused port access to American vessels that were nuclear-powered or capable of carrying nuclear weapons. This meant, in effect, an end to the ANZUS alliance and to the spirit of dependence that had characterised New Zealand foreign policy from the time of European colonisation. While these changes were taking place, another factor was making the face of New Zealand life less unrelievedly European. From the 1960s a second Polynesian migration was taking place. Immigrants came from the Cook Islands (part of New Zealand), the Tokelaus, Niue, Samoa and Tonga. New Zealand cities, especially Auckland, began to hear drums and see lavalavas and to taste fish cooked in coconut milk.

By the 1980s there were more than 80,000 Pacific Islanders living in New Zealand. This fact, along with the existence of some 300,000 Maoris, plus a smattering of Indian and Chinese, led to an awareness of a multi-racial, multi-cultural indentity. The words of a popular television commercial celebrated this identity as 'different faces, many races, living in the sun', voicing the hope shared by most New Zealanders that people from different ethnic backgrounds with differing lifestyles could live the good life in harmony.

By the late 1980s, New Zealanders are far from constituting a single homogeneous culture. But it is possible to make some generalisations about them and about how they see themselves and the world beyond them.

Obviously, almost all New Zealanders speak English. But a considerable number of English words are used in a peculiarly New Zealand fashion: 'panelbeaters' repair the body work of cars, for example; 'metalled' roads are unsealed; paddock, creek and bach mean quite different things to New Zealanders than they do to Englishmen. There are also Maori words which have passed into general usage, like whare, mana and tapu. Although vestiges of regional accents can still be found in Southland (the Scottish influence) and Northland (Dalmatian), New Zealand English is largely uniform and its accent and intonation can be recognised by the practised ear. It sounds flatter than 'English' English, but not as flat as Australian. It is something of a compromise between the two.

The number of Maori speakers was also increasing dramatically in the 1980s as Maori and Pakeha adults enrolled in courses designed to save the language from extinction, and as children attended kohanga reo or language nests, in which pre-school education was conducted entirely in Maori. The prospect that a large percentage of New Zealanders would be bi-lingual in the twenty-first century became a real one.

New Zealanders also share a wide range of attitudes. In many senses the country is still a pioneering one and still influenced by its predominantly farming economic base. It's probably true that most New Zealanders still admire a work of practical accomplishment, like a hydro-electric dam, more than they do a work of art. This emphasis is changing slowly, but even as it does New Zealanders remain a highly practical people who value the capacity to 'do-it-yourself' more than any other industrialised country. On weekends New Zealand homes and gardens crawl with people building, repairing, digging, trimming and generally engaged in the kind of activities that people in other countries might call in tradesmen to do, or not do at all.

Beyond this, New Zealanders are also prone to attempting things they have not done before rather than admit to ignorance or inexperience. The cry 'have a go' is as common in real life as it is in sport. If a New Zealander cannot do something, he or she is likely to learn it in the doing; to master the job on the job. This quality gives New Zealanders an impressive degree of adaptability and optimism, and an almost legendary ability to improvise (it was said of New Zealand soldiers in World War Two that they could do anything with a piece of number eight fencing wire). New Zealanders abroad tend not to be intimidated by authority or class restrictions. They demonstrate versatility and reliability. They have what one English publisher has called, in a sporting image that New Zealanders can understand and appreciate, 'a power behind the scrum', a capacity to meet deadlines, to deliver, to get done what they undertake to do. Hence many New Zealanders who have migrated to the United Kingdom have done disproportionately well in their chosen occupations, their competence and their colonial confidence breaking through the barriers imposed by British fastidiousness.

In the arts, too, the spirit is pioneering. Although some practitioners have chosen to go to Europe and North America, where the conventions are comfortably established and the precedents set, many more have been determined to remain under the harsh glare of New Zealand light and suspicion and carve out the conventions appropriate for a country such as this. One of them, Charles Brasch, described the process:

A new society like our own, still undefined, uncharacterised, unidentified, with no values quite settled and no common ends generally acknowledged, will cast about vainly to know what it thinks and believes until it can see what it unequivocally says or what is said for it; that is, until it is revealed to itself in works of art of its own begetting.

In literature, the visual arts and ceramics and pottery, the efforts to carve out a place for the artist in society have met with considerable acceptance over the past two decades. A growing body of New Zealanders is making a living from the arts and finding an even faster-growing audience with which to communicate. And much of the satisfaction with this situation – for artists and consumers – lies in the very need to search for modes, materials and voices that are appropriate for New Zealand rather than simply a pale reflection of European or American models.

New Zealand has a deserved reputation for hospitality – another off-shoot from pioneer days, perhaps. New Zealanders tend to visit casually, without prior appointment. They offer visitors generous refreshment. They tend to make strangers welcome if they are English-speaking, and they are slowly learning to overcome suspicion of those who are not (for more than a century, of course, few New Zealanders encountered people who were not English speakers). This quality of hospitality is perhaps most emphatically apparent in the homes of people with Polynesian antecedents. Anyone who has stayed in a Maori house and accepted the proverbial 'cup of tea' knows what a groaning table of good things such an invitation may involve. For Polynesians, manuhiritanga – the obligation to make visitors welcome – is one of the strongest values of their culture. A relatively high degree of prosperity has enabled New Zealanders to give material expression to their strong impulse for generosity.

Much has been said by way of disparagement about New Zealand's egalitarianism: that it leads to mediocrity and the grey blanket of sameness. In its best manifestations, however, this quality means that most New Zealanders make strenuous efforts to see that their compatriots get 'a fair go' according to their capacity to contribute to society. It means that most New Zealanders have a sympathy for the underdog. It means too that professors are likely to sit alongside plumbers at rugby matches and exchange views on the game; and that (as has happened) a senior civil servant responsible for overseeing a major publishing programme on New Zealand history and culture is also an expert on the form and pedigree of race horses and contributes a racing column to a local newspaper. There are pockets of elitism in new Zealand life; but the popularity of the myth of social equality mitigates them.

If there are such things as archetypical New Zealanders, they are perhaps people like Inia Te Wiata, the freezing-worker from Ngaruawahia who became a world-renowned operatic bass singer; or the mountaineer Edmund Hillary, resourceful, stimulated by difficult challenges, and led by compassion to build hospitals and schools in Nepal. When Hillary reached the summit of Everest in 1953, New Zealanders felt a surge of pride that this laconic, raw-boned young man had represented his country so creditably. He has continued to do this since that time in ways that are different, but which have brought approval and pride from his countrymen in doses equal to that first acclaim.

The Pakeha view of the New Zealand landscape has changed with the course of the twentieth century. Whereas it was formerly seen as alien and threatening – largely because of its unfamiliarity to British immigrants – it is now viewed as home by the vast majority of three-and-a-half million New Zealanders. Nearly two million of them head for beaches, mountains, rivers and lakes in the course of annual holidays. A growing number are returning to rural and coastal environments to live away from urban tensions. Conservation movements have preserved forests, lakes and beaches that were formerly destined for development and despoliation.

It is difficult to make predictions about New Zealand's future. The movement of official institutions (like those of the education and legal systems) in the direction of Maori things suggests that Polynesian features will become more rather than less noticeable in New Zealand life, and that as New Zealand develops a ceremonial language and ritual of its own they are likely to be Maori-based. Indeed, on State occasions, like the funeral of Prime Minister Norman Kirk in 1974, it was the Maori content above all others that provided dignity, beauty and a truly national voice.

Whatever happens, one thing is certain. New Zealand has been colonised twice: once by the Maori; once by the European. New Zealanders no longer feel colonial, nor do they want to be colonised again as a consequence of the invasion of foreign capital or foreign culture. Whatever future forms New Zealand life takes, they will be determined by New Zealanders from New Zealand ingredients, antecedents and traditions. The country does not seek to be isolated from the rest of the world. But there is a strong determination that it should stand on its own feet and welcome the wider world as an equal partner.

Cable Bay on Doubtless Harbour
provides links with New Zealand's
Polynesian and Pakeha history. It lies
on the route that souls of the Maori
dead were reputed to take to Te
Rerenga Wairua, the Leaping-Off
Place of Spirits, at the northern tip of
the North Island. And the first
telegraph cable to reach New Zealand
from the world beyond, laid from
Norfolk Island, was landed here in
1906.

THE NORTH ISLAND

'In the beginning was the land...'
White Island in the Bay of Plenty, one
of New Zealand's three most active
volcanoes, provides a glimpse down
the corridor of the past. The island's
contours, colours and textures match
those of much of the rest of the
country when its land masses were
being formed from molten material
from the earth's core. There is a
further link with the history of the
country as a whole. It is widely
believed that the canoes of the earliest
Polynesian migrants to New Zealand
made landfall in the Bay of Plenty,
and that steam from the volcano was
responsible for one of the country's
oldest names: Aotearoa, Land of the
Long White Cloud.

A woolshed at Wainui Junction near Kaitaia reflects an orange roof back at the rising sun. This landscape is typical of New Zealand's far north: parched pasture clinging to ancient sand dunes, pohutukawa trees pressed by the weight of wind on a hill-less environment.

The grasses of the Pawarenga Valley provide rich feed for dairy cattle among the remnants of an ancient kauri forest. Here a daughter of the valley's largely Maori community brings in one of the family cows for early-morning hand-milking.

OPPOSITE

Like all rural Maori communities, the people of Pawarenga are bound to the land on which they live by history and spirituality. This church, St Gabriel's, was built at the instruction of a Dutch Mill Hill priest who believed that the houses of God should bear witness on the surrounding landscape. The tenets of Christianity, in this case Catholicism, knitted well with traditional Maori spiritual concepts and virtually the whole community in this area is Catholic.

Inside an adjacent church, Holy Trinity, the marriage of
Maoridom and Christianity is symbolised in the patterns
of the fretwork behind the altar and of the altar rails. The
atmosphere is one of intimacy and peace, the soft light
conducive to meditation and prayer. The name given to
Christianity in the district is Te Whakapono – the
Coming of Light.

A family at worship in St Gabriel's Church, Pawarenga.
In traditional and contemporary Maori cosmology, all
major activities begin and end with karakia or prayer. In
Catholic communities, the Mass is the ritual that brings
the whole village together weekly, and more frequently in
times of death and marriage or on major feast days. The
dark wood of the walls and pews in the body of the
church are characteristic of religious buildings in this part
of the country.

Outside the churches lie the community dead, a constant reminder that contemporary lives are links in a chain of being that stretches into the past, to parents, grandparents, ancestors and gods. The living (and the newly born) are among the dead each time the church is visited. And those dead are remembered and invoked by name whenever a service is held.

Ahipara, at the foot of Ninety Mile Beach, is one of Northland's most active Maori communities. Ceremonial headquarters of Te Rarawa tribe, its huis or gatherings draw Maori people from all over the region. In the early years of the twentieth century it was also a major source of kauri gum and many Dalmatian gum-diggers married into local families. In the 1980s most visitors to Ahipara come for its surf and wind-surfing attractions. This resident, equipped with board, towel and zinc-creamed nose, shows how locals approach water sports.

OVERLEAF Right

Ken Lewis's annual excursion from Parengarenga to Whangarei is the last major cattle drive in the country. The animals are rounded up on stations in the far north and taken to yards at Paua on Parengarenga Harbour. Lewis and his band of drovers then move the 2,000 cattle more than 260 kilometres on foot, a process that takes six weeks.

When Ken Lewis and his drovers arrive at Whangarei
with their cattle, the animals enter the saleyards in
considerably better condition than they would had they
been trucked the same distance.

LEFT

Herekino, a small settlement at the
head of Herekino Harbour, is typical
of Northland communities on the west
coast. While the east side of the region
is known for its white-sand beaches,
booming tourism and low
unemployment, the western
communities are smaller, less
prosperous and largely Maori. They
are a magnet for those who want to
escape the crowds, however. And they
retain many of the features of small-
town life that used to characterise
rural New Zealand as a whole:
intimacy, supportiveness, and a mild
suspicion of strangers.

OPPOSITE

The words beach and bach are linked
by situation and alliteration.
Thousands of New Zealand families
own holiday homes of this kind, most
of them located near the coast. The
basic but functional design and
materials (wood or fibrolite) are said to
constitute New Zealand's single gift to
world architecture. This bach looks
out to sea at Tokerau Beach,
Doubtless Bay, a relatively developed
section of Northland's east coast.

Cheap land, a mild climate and a market created by a transient population of tourists have made Northland a popular location for craft co-operatives. This business, Spectrum Glass, is run by a husband and wife team near Fern Flat. Here they make decorative windows, ornaments, hand-blown glass containers and wind-chimes.

OPPOSITE

Northland is a haven for a range of alternative life-stylers including craftspeople, commune dwellers and survivalists. Barefoot and his companion live in the Victoria Valley, between Mangamuka and Kaitaia. Because their home is a mobile one, however, they are seen frequently throughout the region sampling shops, beaches and congenial camping sites.

Kaitaia, administrative and commercial centre of the far north, pulls in crowds on festival and market days. And when the people gather, so do these Open-air Campaigner gospel singers. Appropriately, the town was founded as a church settlement in 1840 when the first Governor of New Zealand, William Hobson, built an Anglican church there.

OPPOSITE

The Bring-and-Buy is the favourite method of raising money for voluntary activities in New Zealand. In small rural communities in particular it not only takes care of shopping needs but also provides a carnival-like opportunity for people to get together, renew acquaintance and swap local news. This table at Logue's Bush near Warkworth was set up to raise money for the Northland branch of the Royal Forest and Bird Protection Society.

OVERLEAF

The Bay of Islands is the cradle of Pakeha culture in New Zealand. Named by navigator James Cook in 1770, it was successively the site of New Zealand's first township, home of the first British Resident, location for the signing of the Treaty of Waitangi (by which Maori chiefs ceded sovereignty of New Zealand to the British Crown) and the nation's first capital. Today it is Northland's major tourist destination, drawing people in pursuit of history, big-game fishing and maritime scenery.

The Kerikeri Inlet is another historical feature of the Bay of Islands. It is the site of the country's second Anglican mission station, established in 1819. Two buildings survive from mission days: the Kemp house (the oldest building in New Zealand) erected in 1819; and the stone store built in 1833. Across the water stood Kororipo, home of the Ngapuhi fighting chief Hongi Hika. Hongi visited England and Sydney in 1820 and 1821 and returned to Kerikeri with more than 1,000 muskets. He used these to subjugate most other tribes in the North Island and was successful because his adversaries had not yet acquired firearms.

RIGHT

Day-long boat trips around the Bay of Islands are one of the district's most popular tourist attractions. The sheltered character of the bay, enhanced by its shape and its hundreds of islands and islets, means that launches can put to sea more frequently here than in any other part of the country. Trips available include the route formerly used to pick up cream from dairy farmers, fishing expeditions, and this one to Cape Brett to view the lighthouse there and the famous hole-in-the-rock on Piercy Island.

OVERLEAF

For the southward traveller, the first point of contact with and identification of Auckland City is the harbour bridge, spanning the Waitemata from Northcote to Westhaven. Completed in 1959, it opened the city's North Shore to suburban settlement as packed and as popular as that which already characterised the south shore. Across the far horizon lie the Waitakeres, an ancient volcanic range now clothed in bush and protecting West Auckland from west coast winds.

Auckland's reputation as the City of Sails is never more spectacularly confirmed than at the beginning of the New Zealand-South America leg of the Whitbread Round the World yacht race. Not only do the competitors erupt into the Waitemata, but they are accompanied by spectators in some of the 70,000 pleasure craft that Aucklanders are reputed to own (giving the city the highest number of boats per capita of any city in the world). The miracle of this spectacle is not so much the number of boats afloat as the fact that the competitors make it to the harbour entrance without multiple collisions.

Tamaki Bay in summer provides one of the city's popular swimming, boating and sunbathing beaches. If Aucklanders are hedonistic, as other New Zealanders sometimes claim, it is because of the hot climate and easy proximity to safe, white-sand beaches. Many families virtually live on the sand over summer weekends and the Christmas holiday break. Just west of Tamaki Bay along this coast is Okahu Bay, famous historically as the site of an agreement in 1840 between the Ngati Whatua owners of the Auckland isthmus and the first Governor of New Zealand, William Hobson. This meeting resulted in the sale to Europeans of the land that was to become Auckland city, and to the establishment there of the nation's second capital.

In winter the ratio of sports spectators to participants increases, at the expense of the sports themselves. Rugby is not as popular in New Zealand today as it was in the 1950s and 1960s. But it still draws vast crowds in and around Auckland. Some go simply to watch the game; others to share the shiver of excitement that runs through a large live crowd when tries are scored and goals landed. These supporters are gathered at the Counties ground in Pukekohe, South Auckland.

OPPOSITE

Aucklanders at play are more than swimmers and sailors. They are also joggers – on a larger scale than anywhere else in the country or the world. Jogging as a sport began in the city in the late 1950s and spread from there throughout New Zealand, and then to Europe and North America. The Round the Bays fun-run, shown here on Tamaki Drive approaching Okahu Bay, attracts as many as 70,000 entries annually, making it the biggest event of its kind in the world.

ABOVE

ABOVE

Anzac Day was originally established to commemorate the allied landings at Gallipoli on 25 April, 1915. Now it is the day when the nation mourns all its war dead. Here, medalled veterans of World War Two gather around Auckland's major war shrine, the cenotaph at the front of the War Memorial Museum, for the mid-morning service. Although the ranks of former servicemen thin year by year, the numbers attending the city's Anzac Day commemorations do not. There was scarcely a family in New Zealand that did not have a husband or a father fighting in World War One or Two. And the survivors of these families show a continuing inclination to remember that service.

OPPOSITE

If Auckland's major recreational amenity is its beaches, its second asset is its parks, which constitute the 'lungs' of the city. Many of these centre on the region's surviving volcanic cones, of which the largest is One Tree Hill. The reserve in this instance is Cornwall Park, donated to the citizens of Auckland by Sir John Logan Campbell on the occasion of an early Royal Visit to the city. The donor himself lies buried under the obelisk alongside the lone pine at the top of the hill that preserves its Pakeha name. In pre-European times, as Maungakiekie, the group of cones making up the hill was one of the largest Maori settlements in the country.

OPPOSITE

The second largest park close to the city is the Auckland Domain, which also lies around an extinct volcanic crater. In addition to housing the Auckland Museum, the Domain has one of the best collections of plants and trees – native and exotic – in the country. The winter garden, shown here, specialises in flowers and shrubs that bloom during winter months, ensuring that visitors have interesting flora to view the whole year round. It was established by Thomas Cheeseman, one of the country's best-known early botanists.

LEFT Above

Sports too come into the category of successful exotic transplants into New Zealand. The polo ground at Clevedon, south of Auckland, is in constant use throughout the summer. In contrast with players in the United Kingdom, New Zealand enthusiasts include people from all walks of life. The only qualification required is that they love the sport and know how to handle horses. Members of the Royal Family have played on this ground.

LEFT Below

Cricket is another sport that has put down deep roots in New Zealand. In recent years, interest in the game has been fertilised by the popularity of one-day cricket on television, and by the success of the New Zealand team at the highest levels of international competition. Pitches have sprung up all over the country, some permanent, others – like this strip of mown grass at Whitford, south of Auckland – strictly impromptu. In circumstances such as these, new generations of Richard Hadlees chance their arms.

ABOVE

A government-sponsored Come Alive campaign brought back into recreation and sport many adults who had abandoned such activities in their youth. The highly active character of jogging and cricket is not for everybody, though. Gentler forms of exercise, such as yoga, are popular with an older age group. This yoga class is conducted in Albert Park, within metres of Auckland's city centre, as part of a council-sponsored Rhythm of Life festival.

LEFT

A glimpse of life in pioneer times is provided at the Howick Historical Village. This man demonstrates the almost lost art of making bread in camp ovens and billy tea. In the nineteenth and early twentieth centuries, such skills were essential for survival. In the latter part of the twentieth century, they are colourful features of the nation's past. As a bonus, visitors discover that food made in the outdoors over a camp fire has lost none of its taste.

OPPOSITE

The pioneer spirit survives in New Zealand cities – in this case in the suburb of Ponsonby – in the determination of elderly folk to look after themselves. This pensioner attends to her garden three or four days a week and proudly carries out her own household repairs. The tradition of New Zealanders as do-it-yourselfers is a direct link with the country's egalitarian past, in which tradesmen and servants were available only to the very wealthy.

The Henderson Valley to the west of Auckland was the country's first extensive grape-growing and wine-making region. Although the district now produces only 10 per cent of the country's total volume of wine, many of the Dalmatian and Lebanese families who pioneered the industry still operate vineyards there. This man works for Balic Wines, one of a dozen companies open to the public for sightseeing, wine-tasting and buying.

Karangahape Road is Auckland's – and the country's – most culturally diverse street. This Chinese fruit and vegetable shop is only one of dozens that stock food from Asia and the Pacific in addition to less exotic local fare. Customers in this area are likely to include a large proportion of Cook and Niue islanders, Tongans and Samoans – citizens whose ethnic background makes Auckland the world's largest Polynesian city.

ABOVE

Pakeha rituals can sometimes seem restrained alongside the Polynesian commemoration of Christian festivals, however. These Samoan gospel singers praise the Lord at Otara in South Auckland. Samoans make up the largest per capita church-going group in New Zealand and seldom hesitate to bear Christian witness before the wider New Zealand community.

LEFT

The bulk of Auckland's residents are, of course, Pakeha New Zealanders. They too have rituals and festivals every bit as noisy and colourful as those of more recent migrant cultures from Pacific and Asian countries. Here an extended family celebrates Christmas Day at Waimauku, northwest of Auckland. The occasion included songs, speeches, and a four-course dinner served with wine.

OPPOSITE

This Samoan elder, also in Otara, waits for his family to accompany him to church on Sunday. The leis and shell necklaces around family photographs, mat on the floor, and the custom of discarding footwear inside the house are all characteristic of Island homes in New Zealand, as is the presence of the Bible.

ABOVE

Maoritanga, the indigenous culture of New Zealand, is kept alive through a vigorous practice of language, dance and song. These children perform at the cultural festival held annually at Turangawaewae Marae, Ngaruawahia, on the Waikato River. This marae, ceremonial headquarters of the Maori King Movement, is the unofficial Maori 'capital' of New Zealand. The festival is held in conjunction with a hui of loyalty and thanksgiving that celebrates the accession of the Maori Queen, Dame Te Atairangikaahu.

LEFT

Another aspect of Maori culture practised throughout Waikato is taniko, the art of weaving flax. This class at Oparure is taught by Digger Te Kanawa who, with her mother Rangimarie Hetet, has been responsible for a major revival of the craft. The King Movement has encouraged such activities – as a strong expression of Maori identity and as an activity that adds to the cohesion of local Maori communities.

OPPOSITE

The character of the Waikato River as a dwelling-place of spirits is reflected by the number of cemeteries along its banks, including this Pakeha one at Ngaruawahia. The thick mist that rolls off the river and swirls around its sacred places was a further reason for regarding it as a source of spiritual presences.

'Waikato taniwharau, he piko he taniwha,' says an old proverb: Waikato, river of a hundred bends, and on every bend a taniwha or Great Chief. Nowhere are the bends of the river more apparent than at the delta close to where the largest waterway in the country discharges into the Tasman Sea at Waikato Heads. The river is seen by its Maori neighbours as far more than a source of food and a navigable waterway. It is also a repository of the spirits of gods and ancestors and hence is extremely sacred.

Seaside retirement: Jane Millar of Raglan sits behind
lunch and among a lifetime's accumulation of domestic
paraphernalia. Like members of countless Waikato Pakeha
families, she spent 60 years working on a dairy farm, then
moved to the coast with her brothers to season old age
with a view of the sea and the breath of salt air.

Women form the backbone of social life in rural
communities and the Country Women's Institute has
acted as their rallying point for more than 60 years. Here
the CWI establishes an imposing presence in a parade
commemorating the centenary of Cambridge, described in
a promotion brochure as 'a well-laid out town of pleasant
English-looking aspect'.

Farming under pressure: the annual agricultural field days at Mystery Creek near Hamilton provide an opportunity for farmers to let off steam on this graffiti board. The results reveal more anger than wit.

Wood-chopping is a highly regarded feature of recreational life in the central North Island, location of New Zealand's largest millable forests. At right an axeman demonstrates speed and accuracy at Tokoroa in the course of a Waitangi weekend competition, and (opposite below) pine blocks await the attention of further competitors.

Pakeha students are an ethnic minority at this primary school at Maketu in the Bay of Plenty. The town is predominantly Maori and stands near the landing place of the *Arawa* canoe, reputed to have reached the district from Island Polynesia in the fourteenth century. In the nineteenth century the district was the scene of heavy fighting between pro- and anti-government Maori forces. Today Maketu is one of the headquarters of the Arawa tribe.

LEFT

A teacher from Maketu school gives her pupils a spontaneous swimming lesson. As in most coastal communities, children at Maketu are taught to swim at an early age to allow them to use the sea with confidence and safety.

Many New Zealanders also take to the bush wilderness areas with confidence. This trampers' hut is one of dozens available to holiday-makers within the 210,000-hectare Urewera National Park. The park is veined with magnificent tramping and walking tracks.

Lake Waikaremoana in the heart of the Ureweras is acclaimed as the most beautiful lake in the North Island. The name means 'sea of sparkling water'. It is star-shaped and surrounded by bush, and its sheltered arms provide ample opportunities for safe fresh-water boating and for comfortable camping.

Rising up from the inland Bay of Plenty region the Ureweras support a vast stand of mountainous bush that provides the North Island with its largest tract of native forest. The Ureweras were the traditional home of the Tuhoe people who still live there in large numbers around the park boundaries.

White Island in the Bay of Plenty lies at the eastern end of a chain of volcanoes that runs as far as Taranaki on the west coast of the North Island. It is the country's most spectacularly active cone, a scene of boiling pools, steam and gas vents, sulphur holes and acid lakes. The vents shown here are on Donald Mound, named after Donald Pye who disappeared with ten other men about the time of a major eruption on the island in 1914. According to local Maori tradition, White Island was the source of fire.

ABOVE

Waimangu ('Black Waters') is one of the best known thermal regions on the North Island volcanic plateau. Its attractions include the Waimangu Cauldron, a boiling lake that covers more than 10 hectares and is the largest of its kind in the world; and the Warbrick Terrace shown here, named after the region's first professional guide, Alfred Warbrick. Warbrick's brother and three others were killed during an eruption of the famous Waimangu Geyser in 1903. The geyser last erupted in April 1917, destroying the local hotel and an area known appropriately as Frying Pan Flat.

OPPOSITE

With the extinction of the Waimangu Geyser, Pohutu in Whakarewarewa, Rotorua, became the country's best known geyser. It erupts several times a day and rises to a height of more than 18 metres. It is surrounded by an area of silica terraces, hot springs and boiling mud, all of which draw tourists to Whakarewarewa in huge numbers. The process by which Whaka mud throws up thick bubbles which then burst, looking like boiling porridge, is a source of special fascination for visitors.

Mount Tongariro in the centre of the North Island gave its name to the country's first National Park, the region surrounding it, in 1887. The mountain is a volcano, adjacent to the larger cone Ngauruhoe. This view shows the Emerald Lake, one of several on and around the mountain. Although the park is famous primarily as a destination for skiers in winter, it is equally popular with trampers in the summer months.

ABOVE

'Upon the uplands, even striding,' a poet wrote of pylons.
These massive structures march across the Desert Road, a
plateau of high-country tussock which lies to the east of
Tongariro National Park.

OPPOSITE

Lake Taupo, located in the centre of the North Island, is
sometimes referred to as the heart of the Fish of Maui,
Maori name for the North Island. In fact the lake is a
vast volcanic crater which last erupted about 1,850 years
ago, casting ash from North Cape to Cook Strait. The
now-peaceful lake is a popular tourist destination,
particularly in summer. The island on the horizon was
used as a Maori burial site in pre-European days.

Taranaki or Mt Egmont (both names are now accepted officially) dominates the west coast of the North Island. In Maori legend, Taranaki was originally part of the volcanic cluster at the centre of the island. After a falling out with the other mountains, it decided to remove itself to its more isolated location. The Wanganui River is said to mark the route of its migration. The mountain is famous today for its near-symmetrical cone and its resemblance to Japan's Mount Fujiama.

Calves on a Manaia farm, being fattened for eventual disposal as beef, follow their owner and benefactor to the daily source of milk. Some who can't wait are already trying to suck sustenance from his fingers.

OPPOSITE

Taranaki the mountain has also given its name to the area of land dominated by the sight of the peak. That region is well known as the home of some of the country's best dairy and beef cattle. These farmers follow the progress of a cattle auction in Hawera, Taranaki's second largest town.

Taranaki has far more to boast about than cows. Kevin
Wasley's Elvis Presley Memorial Room at his home in
Hawera ('Gracelands') is open to the public and is one
source of a growing number of visitors to the town.
Wasley, a fanatic Presley fan, has been collecting
memorabilia for three decades. The front of his house is
decorated with a mural of Presley's former home in
Memphis, Tennessee.

ABOVE

Throughout the country, particularly in rural districts, travellers come across frequent instances of New Zealand ingenuity that verge on eccentricity. One of the best examples is the Mangaweka Shell Museum. This dairy-tearooms has several rooms densely covered and ornamented with New Zealand seashells. Outside is an Austin 7, believed to be the only car in the world so decorated (or camouflaged).

OVERLEAF

The landscape of Hawke's Bay, shaped by glaciers, was recognised by European colonists in the nineteenth century as promising grand hills for sheep. And, as it transpired, the region rapidly built up considerable wealth from the production and sale of wool and sheep meat. Much of this wealth was initially concentrated in the hands of a small number of station-owning families. The larger stations were broken up by government legislation at the turn of the century, however, and the Hawke's Bay oligarchy has all but disappeared. The region as a whole still prospers from meat and wool, and from crops grown on the plains.

ABOVE

Maize is one of the largest of Hawke's Bay crops and the bulk of it goes towards farm animal feed. Other parts of the region are given over to fruit and vegetables in quantity, for fresh supply to the rest of the country and for preservation at one of Hawke's Bay's canneries. The district attracts workers and harvesting machines from all over the country.

BELOW

Country kids have fewer transport problems than their city counterparts, thanks to horses. This pair dawdle on their way home from school along the southern Wairarapa coast at Palliser Bay. In the nineteenth and early twentieth centuries, Palliser Bay beach was the only route into the Wairarapa district and farmers had to drive their animals around the coast so as to establish their profitable flocks and herds.

HERE LIVES A

RAWLEIGH MAN

A typical New Zealand villa at Sanson, administrative centre of the Manawatu district. Hundreds of thousands of homes were built in this style at the turn of the century and the relatively plentiful supply of timber ensured that they were cheap by world standards. The Rawleigh's sign identifies a representative of one of New Zealand's most ubiquitous companies, which has for years supplied health-related products to New Zealand homes by door-to-door salesmanship.

Hitch-hikers come in all ages, shapes, sizes and sexes, and they take to the road for a multiplicity of reasons. The mission of this traveller can only be guessed at. He was met on the road into Wellington between the hills overlooking Porirua and those that surround Wellington Harbour.

OPPOSITE

The Kapiti coast near Paekakariki is named after the island, which lies along the western horizon like a basking whale. Most of this coast is rugged, the action of the sea influenced by the turbulence of the Cook Strait weather systems a short distance to the south. The island is one of the country's major bird sanctuaries and has – among other species – the last surviving specimens of the little spotted kiwi.

ABOVE

Because of the strong earthquake risk (the city is built on a fault line that shifted twice in the nineteenth century and brought down many of the capital's buildings), much of old Wellington has been pulled down in recent years. The new shops and office blocks deprive long-term residents of their former reference points. But they also give the city a new, fresh-faced aspect, one that is especially popular with overseas visitors.

OPPOSITE

Wellington, the nation's capital, is a harbour city that clings precipitously to sheer hills. A local poet once marvelled that it was the only place in the world where one could drop apple cores down ships' funnels – if one wanted to. Here ribbons of motorway merge into the State highway north, hugging the shoreline and indicating the capital's vulnerability should another one of the region's periodic earthquakes disrupt communications.

OVERLEAF

Wellington city from the heights of Kelburn, looking across the university plateau and down to the reclaimed Aro Flat. Without reclamation, Wellington could never have supported the conglomeration of buildings, businesses and government administrative offices that constitute the life of the city. The harbour is said by locals to be the most beautiful in the world, and its location at the midpoint of the country ensured its importance from the time of European settlement in 1839. The Hutt Valley can be seen in the distance and – behind that – the Rimutaka Ranges separating Wellington from the Wairarapa.

In the heart of Wellington a commuter shades his eyes
from the afternoon sun as he heads for the railway
station. The buildings behind are the Hotel Waterloo, one
of the capital's traditional watering holes, and the national
post office headquarters.

Like Auckland, Wellington is a city of and for immigrants. Thousands of Central Europeans arrived just before and after World War Two. And Pacific Islanders began to make their homes there from the 1960s. This pair, just off the train from Porirua, plan their day in the city from their starting point outside Wellington Railway Station.

If Auckland's hot weather is conducive to hedonism, Wellington's rigorous cold and winds keep people indoors, brooding and breeding culture. Among the capital's best known institutions are the Wellington City Art Gallery, which has acquired a reputation for showing vigorous and innovative painting and sculpture, and the New Zealand School of Dance, which trains future professional dancers.

OPPOSITE

Beyond the Picton Rail Ferry, linking the North to the South Island, Wellington's close juxtaposition of sea, boats and houses is clearly visible. The ferry has a twice-daily service and carries passengers, cars and railways rolling stock. It offers the only commuter boat service across Cook Strait.

ABOVE

Wellington's notorious gale-force winds annoy some and terrorise others. But for windsurfers they simply provide challenges and add spice to their sport. This exponent ploughs the waves at Lyall Bay, while planes land and take off from Wellington's airport only a short distance away.

Not Arab dhows in the Gulf of Aden
but another of Wellington Harbour's
extraordinarily varied faces. These
yachts sail into the late afternoon
from Eastbourne in the east towards
Somes Island at the centre of the
harbour. Yachties claim that if you
cut your teeth sailing on Wellington
Harbour, you will subsequently be
able to handle conditions anywhere in
the world.

The cold beauty of a South Island sunrise, seen from Westport Beach on the West Coast. Names are often signposts to a district's past, and this one was named after Westport in Clew Bay, County Mayo — a relic of the large number of Irishmen who reached the West Coast from Australia in the nineteenth century. The 'port' is the mouth of the Buller River and was formerly famous for its export of high quality coal.

THE SOUTH ISLAND

Looking out from Wellington across Cook Strait towards the South Island. Cook Strait is named after the great British navigator, James Cook, first European to discover that the North and South Islands were separated by this often rough stretch of water. Although the strait is not wide – 17 kilometres at its narrowest point – it constitutes something of a psychological as well as a geographical gap. North and South Islanders have different and clearly defined senses of identity; and most New Zealanders cross the strait only infrequently.

The lengthy Wairau Bar, enclosing Big Lagoon, is one of the most arresting features of the northern South Island. It is more than an oddity of landscape, however. It is also the location of an Archaic Maori campsite that was seasonally occupied more than one thousand years ago. The occupants apparently chased gigantic moas onto the spit and then killed the trapped birds. Canterbury Museum excavations on the bar in the 1940s resulted in the term 'Moa Hunter' being coined to describe those early Polynesian colonists of New Zealand.

This Kaikoura beach is typical of the north-east coast of the South Island: rugged, cold, shingly rather than sandy. The area was a favoured source of seafood for the Maoris in pre-European times and the very name Kaikoura means 'meal of crayfish'. Maori and Pakeha fishermen continue to catch this delicacy off the coast here. But now more of it goes to North America than to feed New Zealanders.

ABOVE

Havelock lies on the innermost arm of the Marlborough
Sounds, named by James Cook in 1770. It is a sheltered
waterway, ideal for bathing, fishing and swimming.
Pakeha settlers were originally attracted here by a gold
rush at nearby Wakamarina in 1864, and the Nobel Prize-
winning physicist Ernest Rutherford spent most of his
boyhood in Havelock.

OPPOSITE

Water and sand swirl to concoct marble-like patterns at
the entrance to the Parapara Inlet in Golden Bay. True to
its name, Golden Bay has an abundance of yellow-sand
beaches. In 1642 it was the scene of the first known
contact between Maori and European. Dutch navigator
Abel Tasman lost four men here in a clash with local
inhabitants after the Maoris had mistaken his blowing a
trumpet for an invitation to fight. Tasman called the area
Murderers' Bay, a name that was changed by later settlers
who disliked its bloody connotations.

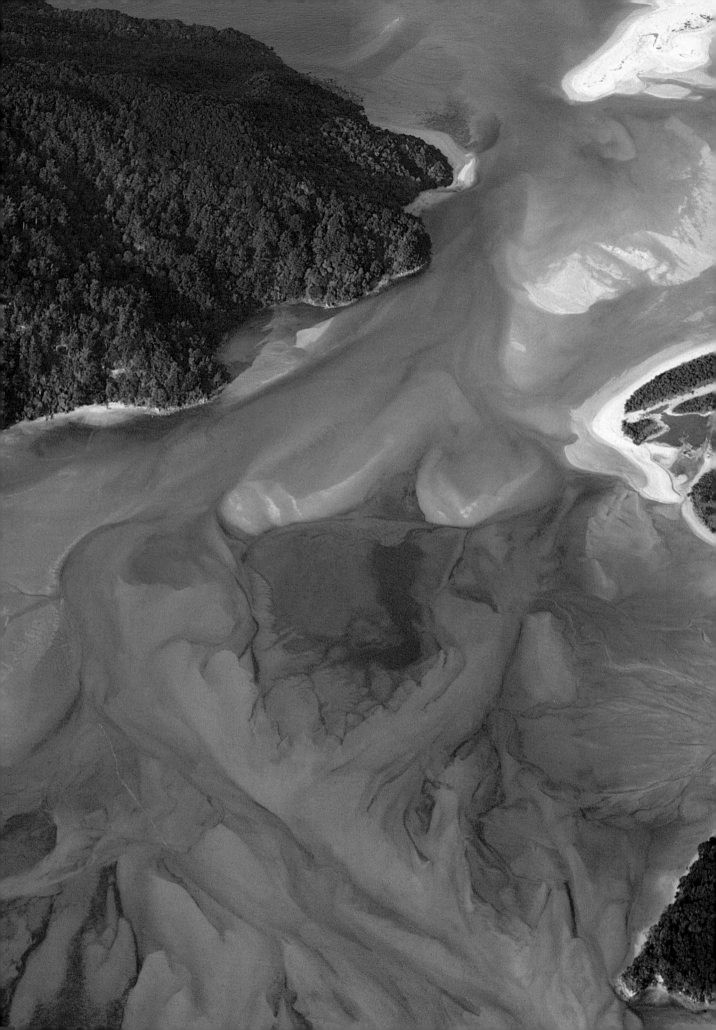

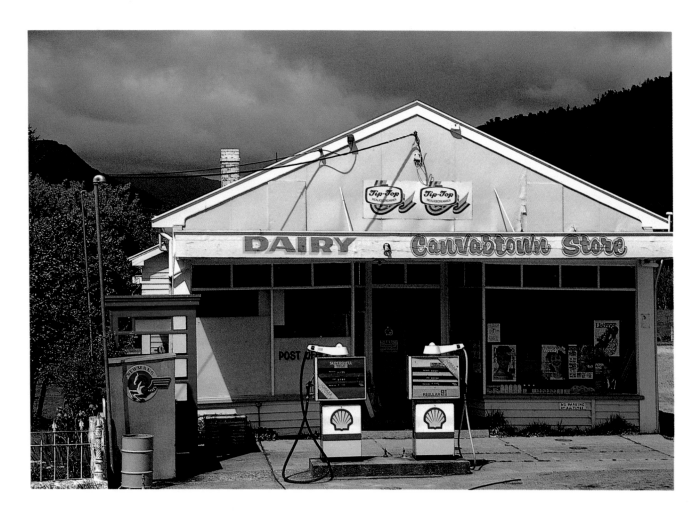

ABOVE

Canvastown, inland from the Marlborough Sounds, stood on the edge of the Wakamarina goldfield and serviced it in the 1860s. In those days it was a feverish scene of hotels, dance halls, stores and drunken revelry. Now it is a quiet hamlet on the Blenheim-Nelson road and a venue for campers in summer.

LEFT

In winter, Canvastown residents emulate the example of thousands of other country folk and play rugby – to keep fit, to keep warm, and to create a sense of occasion on otherwise empty weekends. These teams of school-aged youngsters leap for the ball as the sun disappears behind the high hills to the south of the township.

The West Coast of the South Island has been called a country within a country. The landscape is different from anywhere else (hilly and rugged, with narrow lowlands close to the sea). Communities are small but strong, hospitable but fiercely loyal to the Coast. Much of the inhabitants' quality of sturdy independence dates from the days of gold and coal mining. Blackball, seen here as the early morning sun strikes a local backyard, is a typical West Coast township. It survived the gold boom of the 1860s to move into the coal era; and when that finished the population dwindled. A core of loyal residents remains.

ABOVE

West Coasters are seldom guilty of predictability. This Greymouth couple chose to pose for their wedding photographs in the town's railway yards, escorted by Toyota trucks (ideal for the district's notoriously rough roads). The rail link between Greymouth and Christchurch is the transport artery in and out of the Coast. The port of Greymouth – really only an occasionally navigable river mouth – has declined sharply in importance in the twentieth century.

OPPOSITE

Denniston was a coal town, with three mines adjacent to the settlement. Like much of the West Coast it is now derelict, the relics of busier years clinging to the hills like ghosts of a lost civilisation. When the mines closed, the residents moved some kilometres away to the junction town of Waimangaroa.

A characteristic West Coast shoreline: battered rocks, a cold and turbulent Tasman Sea. This section of the New Zealand coast was responsible for more shipwrecks than any other in the nineteenth century as vessels trying to service the gold-mining communities came to grief on the inhospitable shore.

West Coast forest is often a mixture of rimu and beech, as in this segment of bush near Charleston. In recent years this resource has been the focus of fierce fighting between conservation groups, who prefer to reserve remaining forests for tourism and recreation, and a section of Coast residents who want to continue to earn a living from milling native timber.

ABOVE

Punakaiki between Greymouth and Westport is famous
for its blowholes and pancake rocks. A headland of
stratified limestone has been ground away by wind and
sea into fantastic shapes. Some of them resemble giant
pancakes laid one on top of the other. When the sea is
heavy, the whole area is alive with rumblings, roarings
and hissings as waves race through subterranean channels
and burst out of the vents. Unexpectedly, one of the
Coast's few safe swimming beaches is located a short
distance to the north.

OPPOSITE & OVERLEAF

The Franz Josef (opposite) and Fox glaciers, within a few
kilometres of one another, are among the last of hundreds
of great tongues of ice that formerly pushed their way
down from the heights of the Southern Alps into the
Tasman Sea. Almost all have now disappeared, including
those that formed the spectacular fiords on the south-west
coast. These two too were in retreat until recently, but
there is still more than sufficient ice left to attract and
delight visitors to the Coast.

Christchurch, New Zealand's flattest city, sprawls across the Canterbury Plains. Founded in 1850 as an Anglican settlement, it is more English-looking than other New Zealand communities. It has a town square with a cathedral, the River Avon meanders through it with tree- and flower-lined banks, it has spacious parks, and it is well known for the beauty of its private gardens. Behind the city, to the west, the Southern Alps hang like a curtain.

Christ's College, a privately endowed institution founded
in the nineteenth century and based on English public
school principles, matches the character of the city of
Christchurch. Even its physical aspects – its stone walls,
slate roofs and quadrangles – are reminiscent of English
antiquity. The college's sense of tradition is enhanced by a
series of rituals, one of which is the daily turning of a
page in a book containing the hand-written names of all
the old boys who lost their lives in World War One. In
spite of a strong system of State education in New
Zealand, private schools continue to thrive – they more
than doubled in number between 1930 and 1980.

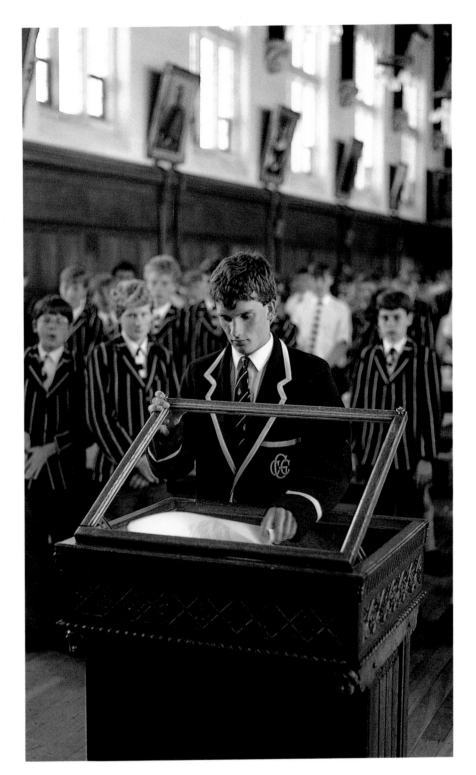

ABOVE

New Zealanders' growing interest in and valuation of their past is reflected in this tobacconist's shop at Ferrymead on the outskirts of Christchurch. Bric-a-brac that would once have been thrown away as junk is now finding a place in New Zealand homes, in antique shops and in businesses that cater for tourists. Ferrymead's other nostalgic attractions include a museum of science and industry, a railway and a tram track.

OPPOSITE

Christchurch is a city of bicycles – thanks to its terrain and the provision of cycle tracks around the parks. These commuters on their way to work on a winter's morning would look equally at home in England's Oxford or Cambridge.

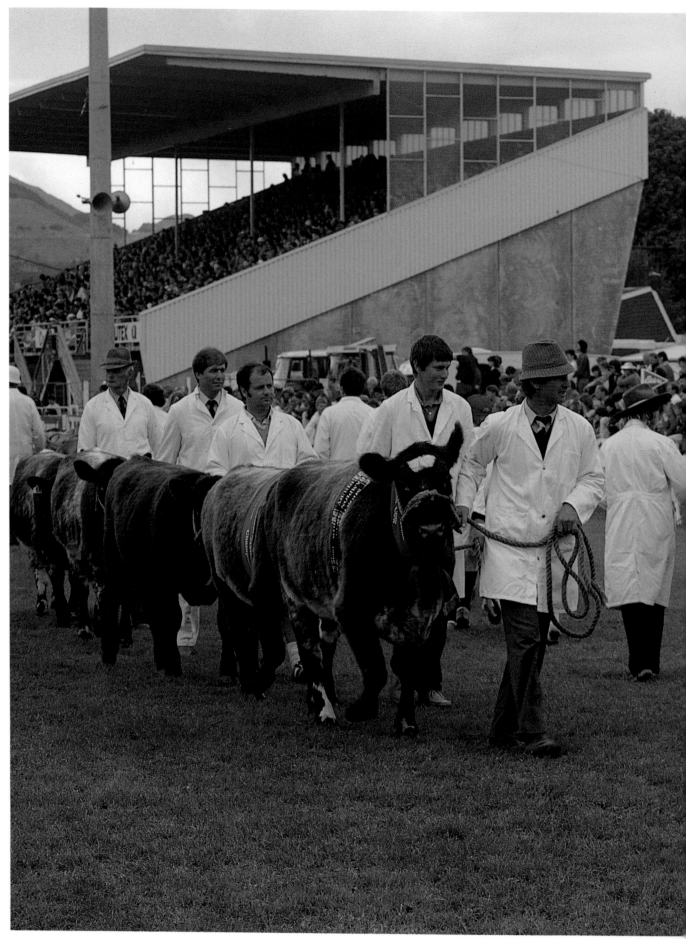

Annual Agricultural and Pastoral shows are major social and business events in towns and cities that service rural areas. They provide an opportunity for suppliers of farm machinery to display their wares, and for animal owners to show off their pets and their best stock. This Christchurch A&P show includes a competition for dogs and a parade of prize-winning animals.

OPPOSITE

The rolling hills of South Canterbury make up one of the country's best sheep-raising districts. At Tabletop Station on the northern banks of the Waitaki River, this rousie takes a break from heaving fleeces and cleaning the shearing shed. In New Zealand, women have always been as much in evidence at shearing time as men, and – traditionally – they do everything except the actual shearing.

The wide golden tussock valleys between the South Island
mountain ranges came to be called the MacKenzie
Country for the Scottish shepherd McKenzie who
allegedly took stolen flocks through the region in the
1850s. Yet another reminder of the close associations of
South Canterbury with Scotland is the local town of
Fairlie, named by a settler David Hamilton because of its
resemblance to Fairlie in Scotland.

Country rituals live long in South Canterbury. Here, in this Waimate living room, friends of a bride-to-be gather for a wedding shower. Such occasions, the women's equivalent of the stag party, are designed traditionally to prepare the bride for domesticity, and guests bring gifts appropriate for that role.

The Fairlie A&P Showgrounds, coated with winter snow.

Sheep are the main source of income for farmers on the hills surrounding Fairlie, as they were 120 years ago. In winter the resemblance to the Scottish landscape is even more marked than at other times of the year.

Down the centre of the South Island the spine and ribs of its mountain ranges are clearly apparent from the air. This view looks across the McKerrow Range into Lake Hawea; and north to Mount Cook, the highest peak in the country at 3,764 metres, on the far horizon.

Pukaki is one of the most attractive of the South Island's narrow glacier-formed lakes. Oddly, the process that created it is not too far removed from the Maori legend that it was scoured out by the adze of Rakaihautu, a god-like ancestor. At the head of the lake stands Mount Cook, foremost target for New Zealand and foreign mountaineers.

The Ahuriri River, which flows out of mountains, through tussock basins and into the headwaters of the Waitaki River, looks like a lake where it moves slowly through flat valleys.

A lone poplar in tussock beside Lake Te Anau is solitary evidence of the European colonisation of this part of the country. Te Anau and its neighbour Lake Manapouri are among the most beautiful of the South Island lakes and have been zealously protected by conservationists from the detrimental consequences of hydro-electric development.

Lake Benmore, for all its grace and beauty, is man-made.
It was formed by the damming of three rivers that flow
into the Benmore Valley. The resulting raising of the
water level created power for electricity generation,
additional water for irrigation schemes and a lake that has
become a major South Island boating playground.

OVERLEAF

The Benmore hydro-electric dam, the
largest in the country.

The road to Alexandra from Wanaka cuts through typical
South Island high country tussock under the lee of the
Dunstan Mountains.

ABOVE

The Roxburgh highway in the heart of
Otago parallels the upper reaches of
the Clutha River and leads to the
Roxburgh hydro-electric station. Until
the building of the Benmore Dam, this
was the largest dam in the country.

OVERLEAF

An early poem about the Cromwell
Gorge highlighted its 'rock floor and
shining cliffs above an unquiet
stream', and described a hawk 'in a
gem-hard sky, gliding down the hot
tired corridor'. Time has not changed
the relative inhospitality of the gorge's
landscape. But irrigation has allowed a
green carpet to spread across the 'rock
floor'.

North of Cromwell the beauty and bleakness of the Otago mountain valleys is apparent at Bendigo, an old goldfield named after its sister field in Australia. Bendigo, Otago, produced little wealth, however, and little warmth. In winter its claims were amongst the hardest to work in the world and many miners perished in this district from exposure. The view is from a miner's abandoned stone cottage.

A rare conjunction of New Zealand farming with the international jet set. The annual Queenstown Dog Derby is held on the ski slopes high above the town, and sheep and cattle dogs are put through their paces on the snow. Dog owners dress much as they do down on the farm, with the addition of a sponsor's numbered T-shirt. Sartorial elegance is achieved by swagger rather than costume co-ordination.

LEFT Above & Below

'Some take delight in the carriages arollin', Others take delight in the curlin' and the bowlin',' according to the old song. These folk take delight in the curling, at Alexandra.

OPPOSITE

A kind of bowls played on ice with heavy stones, curling was brought to Otago in the nineteenth century by Scottish settlers. It is still played throughout the region in winter, largely by the descendants of the Caledonians, and is one of those features of life devised to make changes in season a source of anticipation rather than something to dread.

ABOVE

Another seasonal sport in the far south – this one reserved for spring – is whitebaiting. Here an experienced exponent of this activity, which some describe as more of an art than a sport, swings his scoop net from the Mataura River to investigate a catch. The fish, a juvenile form of the fresh-water species *Galaxias maculatus,* swim up-river in shoals after hatching in tidal estuaries. They make delicious eating and fetch high prices in city fish shops and restaurants.

LEFT

This whitebaiter and his companion, also on the Mataura River, have their own shelter. It allows them to gather strength between stints on the river bank and to entertain fellow fishermen. Such elaborate bivouacs are part of the culture surrounding whitebaiting in the South Island.

In many respects Dunedin seems a city which time has bypassed: it retains its Victorian and Edwardian buildings and homes, and commercial activity has declined here over a period when it has increased in other metropolitan centres. This very decline, however, has brought Dunedin into contact with other features of modern city life, particularly industrial action. Here a union member seeks support for a picket on the city streets.

BELOW

The Moeraki boulders on the coast north of Dunedin are one of the region's more spectacular natural oddities. Many explanations have been given for the existence of these spherical rocks, as large as four metres in circumference. An overseas researcher has claimed they are evidence of visits to earth by extra-terrestrial beings. Maoris identify them as petrified food baskets brought to New Zealand on one of the ancestral canoes. The geological explanation is that they were formed in the sea bed some 60 million years ago by the accumulation of lime salts around a small centre. They crash from an eroding cliff behind the beach as soft coastal mudstone weathers away.

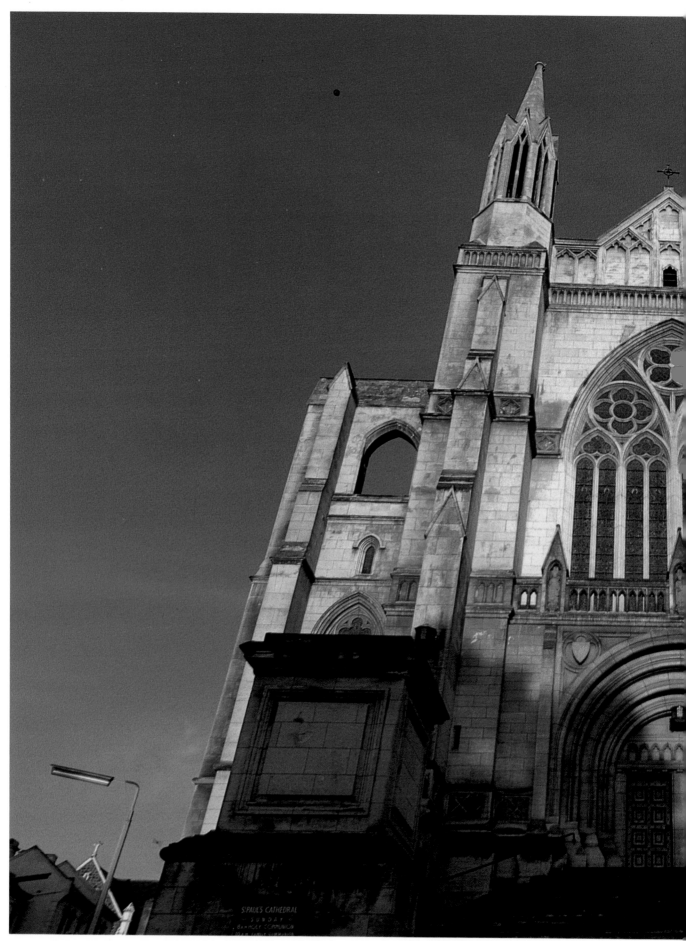

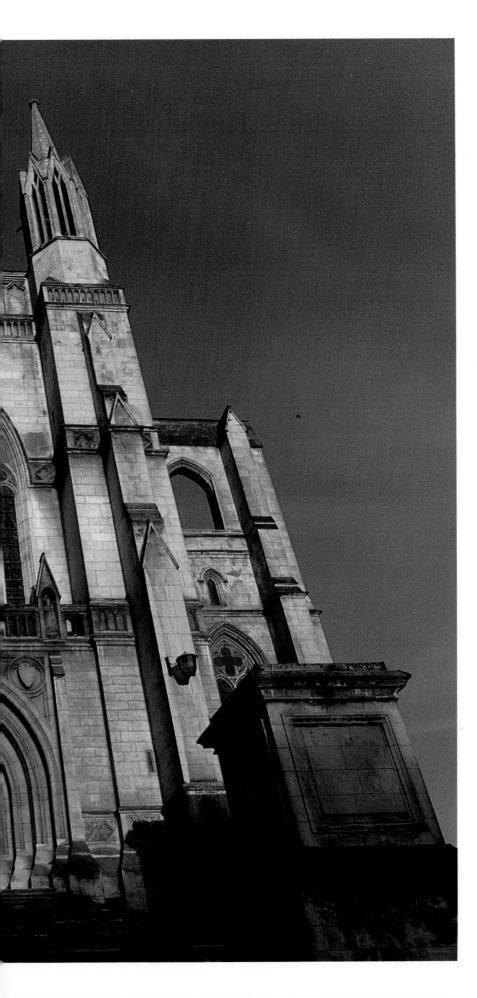

Dunedin's character is nowhere more apparent than in the architecture and materials of its civic buildings. Here St Paul's Anglican Cathedral, built of Oamaru stone at the turn of the century, dominates the city's octagon. Although the original inhabitants of the district were Scottish and Presbyterian, large numbers of English and Irish immigrants followed and brought with them other faiths and other traditions.

OPPOSITE Above

Larnach's Castle is a symbol of Dunedin's prosperity in the nineteenth century, sparked by the discovery of gold in Otago in the 1860s. Work on the castle began in 1871. It was built for and named after local member of parliament William Larnach, who became Colonial Treasurer, Minister of Public Works and Minister of Mines. His own fortunes declined with those of his home city, however, and he committed suicide in parliament in 1898.

OPPOSITE Below

Southland survives on its rural economy but no longer prospers. This Lumsden stockyard and woolshed with its fading advertisement are typical of the mildly derelict look of much of the region's farms and communities. Lumsden itself lies at the foot of the Hokonui Hills, famous in earlier years as a source of moonshine whisky.

ABOVE

Riverton, a comfortably established but small-scale township on the shore of Foveaux Strait, is the oldest Pakeha settlement in Southland and the second oldest in the country. Sealers from New South Wales working the Fiordland coast were calling in here for replenishment of supplies from the end of the eighteenth century. In 1836 a shore whaling station was established on the site of the present town.

OVERLEAF

Otago Harbour is scarcely visible behind the molten turbulence of a sunset into low cloud. The length of Otago Peninsula and the size of the hills to the north of the harbour combine to provide the best anchorage on the southern coast of New Zealand. It was the major factor in the choice of a site for the city of Dunedin in the 1840s.

Fiordland National Park is the country's largest and most rugged. It is made up of mountain ranges, deep glacial valleys running to the sea, and rain forest in between. This view of the park looks westward towards the ocean early in winter, when snow dusts the ranges.

OVERLEAF

From the time of the earliest European settlement of New Zealand, commentators have been struck by the immense geographical variety within what is – by world standards – a small country, and by the grandeur of South Island scenery, exemplified here by Mitre Peak in Milford Sound. The sublimity of such scenery had already given rise to the Maori legend that the gods had placed sandflies there to bite people and prevent their becoming entranced by the beauty of what lay before them.

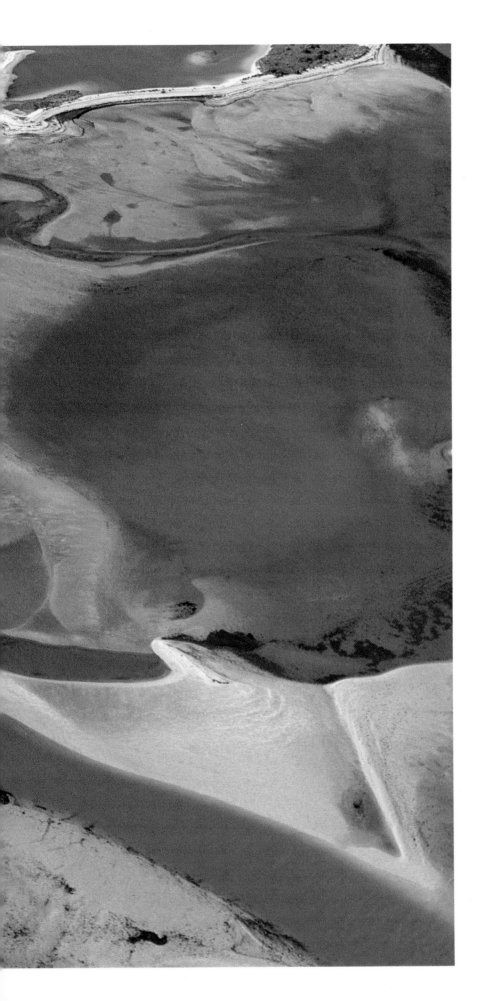

The sand bar at Bluff, a weird swirl of natural patterns, lies at what is literally the bottom of the South Island. From here the oyster boats leave for their seasonal harvesting of the Bluff oyster, the country's best-known shellfish. Apart from Stewart Island, off to the south-west, there is nothing but sea between this stretch of coast and the frozen continent of Antarctica.

One of the dozens of 'cribs' or holiday cottages in Halfmoon Bay, Stewart Island. The collection of buoys at the front is an indication of the amount of flotsam and jetsam that Foveaux Strait currents sweep in to the bay. Most of the residents on the island belong to fishing families with boats anchored off the settlement of Oban in Halfmoon Bay. There is little else from which to earn a living here. Timber was milled on the island until the turn of the century, and tin and gold were mined for a time at Port Pegasus. Now Oban is the only part of the island with a permanent settlement and the population rarely exceeds 300.

Some Statistics

GEOGRAPHY

New Zealand is an archipelago occupying an area of 268,112 square kilometres. It is made up of three main islands: the North Island (114,669 sq.km); the South Island (149,883 sq.km); and Stewart Island (1,746 sq.km). There are dozens of smaller islands totalling 1,814 sq.km in area. From Cape Reinga at the north of the North Island to Bluff at the south of the South Island the country stretches over 1,600 kilometres. It is largely mountainous with less than a quarter of the land lying below 200 metres above sea level. The characteristically hilly and rugged landscape of the North Island is studded with volcanoes, of which some (Ruapehu, 2,797 metres, Ngauruhoe, 2,290 metres) are active; most (including Taranaki, 2,518 metres) are dormant. Thermal activity occurs extensively through the centre of the island and small earthquakes are experienced each year. The larger South Island is dominated by its Alps, of which the highest peak (Mount Cook) is 3,764 metres high and at least 223 other named peaks exceed 2,300 metres. Flanking the Southern Alps on their eastern side is the extensive Canterbury Plain, the largest lowland area in the country.

CLIMATE AND WEATHER

New Zealand lies between Lat. 34°S and Lat. 48°S. Although it is subject to predominantly westerly winds from the Southern Hemisphere's temperate zone, the north of the country extends into the sub-tropical zone. The climate is typically oceanic. Winds blow onto the islands from all directions and can cause sudden changes in the weather. The average temperature in February is 20°C in Auckland and 13°C in Invercargill. The averages in July are 11°C and 5°C respectively. Rainfall is abundant and falls relatively uniformly over the North Island (700–1,500 mm a year). In the South Island, however, it falls mainly to the west of the Alps and in the south-west (more than 8,000 mm a year) and the east is very dry in parts (less than 600 mm a year). In winter snow falls in the mountainous areas of both islands and for a few days on the lowlands to the east of the main divide in the South Island, sometimes even lying at sea level.

PLANTS AND ANIMALS

New Zealand's geographic remoteness and long isolation from other land masses resulted in the evolution and survival of many distinctive species of plants and birds. The plants include tree ferns and conifers such as the kauri. The only large remaining area of virgin bush in the North Island is the Urewera National Park. In the South Island, Fiordland National Park encompasses over one million hectares of dense native beech forest in the south-west of the island. Among the animals are the tuatara, the only surviving member of the dinosaur family, and three species of native frog, none of which has a free-swimming tadpole stage like most frogs. They develop mostly within a gelatinous capsule until hatching as fully-formed froglets. There are more than 250 species of birds including flightless forms such as the kiwi and the rare kakapo, a ground-dwelling parrot. The only indigenous mammals were those of the sea, and bats. Polynesian settlers brought rats and dogs, and Europeans brought animals such as rats, cats, possums and deer, which have threatened the survival of native fauna.

HISTORY

In about AD 800 the first people, Polynesians from Eastern Polynesia, began to settle the country. By the eighteenth century their numbers had swollen to an estimated 100,000 to 120,000 and they had evolved a sophisticated neolithic culture known now as Classic Maori. The first European to sight New Zealand is believed to have been Abel Janzoon Tasman in 1642, although he did not land. Englishman James Cook circumnavigated the country in 1769 and 1770, and was followed by Frenchmen Jean de Surville in 1769 and Marion du Fresne in 1772. From the end of the eighteenth century whales, seals, timber and flax attracted ships from Europe and North America. Sailors and missionaries were the first Pakeha settlers, and organised European colonisation began in 1839. In the following year the Treaty of Waitangi resulted in the country being annexed by Britain. New Zealand became internally self-governing in 1852. The gold rushes and wars between Maori and Pakeha in the 1860s were followed by intensive agricultural development, the establishment of overseas markets for primary produce and bold social reforms. The twentieth century has seen the gradual emergence of a distinct national identity, forged initially through New Zealand's involvement and success in international sporting contests and wars and cemented, since the Depression of the 1930s and World War Two, by a growing literary and artistic culture and an increasingly independent stance in international affairs.

POLITICS AND POPULATION

New Zealand is a parliamentary democracy within the British Commonwealth, with many elements of a welfare state. The head of state is Queen Elizabeth II, represented in New Zealand by the Governor General. The New Zealand Parliament, based in Wellington, has a single house of 97 seats, to which members are elected every three years. Four of those seats are reserved for Maori members, although Maoris can also contest general seats. The two major political parties are Labour and National and there are several smaller parties including the New Zealand Democratic Party, Mana Motuhake Party and the New Zealand Party. The population of the country (1985) is 3.3 million, concentrated overwhelmingly in the North Island, which has some 2.4 million inhabitants as opposed to the South Island's 0.8 million. More than three-quarters of New Zealanders live in cities, of which the largest are Auckland (825,200), Wellington (318,100), Christchurch (289,400), Dunedin (104,600) and Hamilton (103,800).

MAORIS AND PACIFIC ISLANDERS

New Zealand Maoris now number about 279,000 and Pacific Island immigrants about 89,000. Between 1769 and 1896 the Maori population was greatly reduced from its estimated peak of 100,000–120,000 to 42,000 by disease, alcohol, musket warfare and low morale. Maori numbers then recovered steadily as Maoris acquired immunity and adopted sanitation. Today Maoris survive as a result of the controlled accommodation of Pakeha elements into their lives. Beneath Western clothes, technology and other external forms a Maori spirit is expressed through values, extended families, communal organisation, ritual and protocol. The material culture – carving, action songs, weaving – has undergone a revival in the twentieth century. Pacific Islanders too have been contributing to the evolution of a new New Zealand culture since they began to immigrate in large numbers from the 1960s.

AGRICULTURE, FORESTRY AND INDUSTRY

New Zealand's principal agricultural activity is raising animals. Sheep number about 69 million, beef cattle 4.5 million and milking cows 3 million. There are some 76,000 farms occupying about 21 million hectares. Since the Depression of the 1930s New Zealand has been replacing indigenous forests with exotic pines, which mature for felling and use as timber and wood pulp in just over two decades. The proportion of natural to man-made forest is about 6.2 million hectares to 1 million hectares.

Wool, meat and dairy products still provide over half New Zealand's export earnings (56%) but in the 1980s manufactured goods, including forestry products, have risen from 16% to 28% of total export income.

Minerals are scarce in New Zealand, one of the factors which has led to the country's heavy dependence on agriculture and forestry. There are, however, economic quantities of iron ore, extracted from the North Island's West Coast volcanic sand, oil and natural gas, drilled along the Taranaki coast, and coal, mined in both islands, all of which contribute to the country's industrial output.

The country's electricity is obtained mainly from hydro-electric schemes constructed on the lakes and rivers on the eastern flanks of the main divide in the South Island and the Waikato River in the North Island, as well as from locally-supplied natural gas, coal and geothermal stations in the North Island.